Diamond in the Rough

Pieces from My Life

Doris D. Jones

Copyright ©2021 Doris D. Jones

All rights reserved. No part of this publication may be reproduced, distributed, or transmitted in any form or by any means, including photocopying, recording, or other electronic or mechanical methods, without the prior written permission of the publisher, except in the case of brief quotations embodied in critical reviews and certain other noncommercial uses permitted by copyright law.

ISBN-978-1-951300-09-8

Liberation's Publishing LLC ~ West Point, MS. 39773

Diamond in the Rough

Pieces from My Life

Doris D. Jones

Table of Content

Reflection 1

Death of Innocence 3

What Used to Be 5

Golden Shovels 7

Play That Song for Me 9

Sleep On 11

A Day to Remember 13

Time for a Change 17

Journey's End 23

Grandma's Table 27

The Living Dream A Short Story 31

    The Dreams 31

    Northern Light's Poolside 35

    The Meeting 51

    In Love 61

    Big Bro, Lil Bro 75

Back to Business 99

The Aftermath 111

In the News 117

Doris Jones

Reflection

Looking back at my life, one thing stands out, the struggle. Learning how to make do with a little of nothing and be thankful for the crumbs from others table was hard. I grew up in a harsh environment. There was physical, mental, and sexual abuse. This type of environment teaches you to use the most primal survival skills.

I remember watching mom get up at three o'clock in the morning everyday to walk to work. She worked at the Columbus city courthouse. No matter the weather she was always there. Every day like clockwork she was there regardless of the weather getting it in.

I remember seeing her wrap her hands in old socks to stay warm. Her shoes were running over from walking so many miles. I didn't understand at first, but time and error have shown me that she did what she knew to do for her children. It was her way of showing us she loved us the only way she knew how.

I ended up doing the same thing for my

children, following in her footsteps. Just like we took mom for granted my children did the same to me, take me for granted. I worked to provide a better life than I was able to afford as a child. My mom showed me that having children was a full-time job that you wanted to do, because the reward was priceless. The heartache and pain of a childbirth was only a prelude of what was to come, yet it's more than worth the indescribable joy and pride. When you can see how well they turn out.

July twenty-fifth nineteen eighty, I found a reason to live and to strive. His name is Alandrew Ed Rodrick Jones, He was five ponds and three ounces, red wrinkled and squirming. The true beginning of my adult journey. I wasn't alone anymore. I had someone to love me.

Death of Innocence

No rolling hills or babbling brooks, shady glens to relax in or ponds to swim in.

When did the scales fall from my eyes, to see this world for what it is inside?

Cruel, callus, cold to the touch. No life worth living no one cares very much.

Used up thrown around from pillar to post hopeless, hapless gullible fool to waster.

To devour, destroy and decay everything it's given, just to gladly watch hope shrivel and die.

Not one to tell the truth, but this, "Oh, yes we care, just not about you." Young hopeful hearts open with ease setting itself up real nice and easy to squeeze.

Squeeze, squeeze, squeeze, the love, the laughter, the joy of life out of you. Left destroyed, destitute, empty of love and the desire to live.

Oh, and You! Standing there so intelligent, pompous, and proud, wise but not seeing or understanding the role you play in my infinite demise.

This place we live is not what it seems. There is no more good in this life of broken dreams, denied hopes and silent screams.

What Used to Be

I can see the lingering shadows in the doorway

    Or what used to be?

Is that the sound of children's laughter in the yard?

    Or what used to be?

Watch the young men strut like peacocks seeking the attention of the young ladies as they stroll by the church

    Or what used to be?

What used to be a meeting place for women to meet and talk about their issues and life. They talked about their children, their husbands, the struggles of being a wife

    Or what used to be?

Maybe, just maybe the stairs led to a church that would fill up every worship day. The priest in his holy garment passed through the graceful arches to give the word at the alter

    Or what used to be?

Doris Jones

Golden Shovels

When Life Hurts, God Can Heal

Can anyone remember the exact time when?

the joy of living was ripped from life,

Leaving only emptiness, sorrows, and hurts?

All hope is lost except for the grace of God,

Even if He doesn't know that He can

through it all believe that he can Heal.

Come Dance with Me

Gather all your tears and come

I can lighten your burden with dance.

It's not that hard, just take a chance with

Singing, laughter, and dance with me

Play That Song for Me

I pass him by every day.

He plays his sax with such feeling.

I can feel each mournful not, that flows through my veins

Exposing my longings to this cold ass world.

I try to act unaffected, but the tap of my feet,

and the sway of my hips gives me away.

I look at him shyly, he gives me a knowing smile then,

proceed to do a boogaloo that starts my blood pounding.

Oh, there he stands all dolled up, he's a cake-eater

That I can't resist.

Oh, play that song for me, you know the one I like.

The one that makes me move like a wanton hussy getting in a lather.

Hitting all sizes then a bad 2, 5, 1.

Got me two-stepping and side-swaying gyrating madly to his mystical elixir.

Play that song for me, that takes me to another time and place.

Making love to my soul like there is no tomorrow,

only to leave me wanting more consumed with sorrow.

The sweet mad melody takes me to an explosive climax unheard

What can I say?

The man gives me an edge, turn me into a floor-flusher with a single note

So, play that song for me Daddy, you know the one that I like.

A sly wink of his eye lets me know he might.

Sleep On

Being bornin the world piss-pot poor takes away all innocence the moment your feet hit the floor. No one cares about the nappy headed child. Her hopes and dreams hide behind a shy tearful smile.

"Keep ya head down and yo back straight!" That's what was told to me, and I did just that until I was grown.

Now that I'm old I sit back and think, "Only by the grace of God I'm not sic feet under." Raising hell from the day I learned what was what. Never thinking twice about putting my foot on a bitch's throat. My blade was my friend and there was none better.

After a while I had to put her down. I can't keep doing what I'm doing with babies around. Tried to be good, but it didn't last for long. Another bad decision and dogged out again. Bring on the humiliation. Bring on the pain. Let the tears flow, dress me in shame.

I have to keep on fighting with this bitch inside of me to keep her asleep. Going through all I have she really wants out. I cannot take that chance now with grandkids about. It's not easy to do, to keep her asleep.

So back the hell up and don't fuck with me. Just let the bitch sleep.

Sleep on bitch! Sleep on!

A Day to Remember

"What'cha think we waiting for?" Carla asked nervously. I shrugged my shoulder and grunted. She pokes me in the rib with her elbow.

"What we go do? I know they waiting to jump us," she whined.

Turning on her angrily, I snapped back, "If it wasn't for you; we wouldn't be here playing hide and see with those idiots!"

I stomped down the pathway to a tree about a hundred yards ahead of us. Knowing my older sister's habit of getting into messes, I planned for this.

Earlier that morning I hid a couple of bats on the pathway. Carla had gotten me in trouble three time this year and I was not going to get another ass whopping for nobody.

The pathway was a large, wooded area that went from the housing projects backyard and ended at the middle school's playground. I was just tired of fighting, and today I was going to put a stop to it.

"Now I got my ass whopped for you twice- no… three times already. Once for fighting for you, then again for not fighting. I let them bitches beat my ass. Well, I figure if I got to get my ass whooped, I may as well earn it."

The Smith sisters were bad about bullying. They were twice the size of the other kids in school. Brenda was the oldest and looked like a linebacker. Her younger sister Betty Jean looked like a bearrilla. Their two cousins were only there because they were afraid of Brenda. They were all over two-hundred pounds.

Even though I was small, four feet six barely a hundred pounds, I knew how to defend myself and my sister. You didn't grow up with five brothers and not know how to fight. Now I don't know what happed with Carla. She just wanted to have friends so bad, she picked the wrong kind of people.

"This morning, I hid some bats behind a couple of trees. We going to run down, grab them bats and swing for the damned fences. You hear me? If you don't knock one of them bitches out, I'm go beat your ass." Carla nodded her head.

Lord, Carla was five-five with legs that went on forever. She was just hungry for friendship I grabbed her arm and we charged down the path. Tree branches and limbs scratched our faces, but we didn't care. We were on a mission. Giving them plenty of warning that we were coming they blocked the pathway. Grabbing up them bats we started swinging. The satisfying feel of that bat connected with body parts was worth the ass whooping I knew was coming.

Looking around I see Carla whooping one chile like she had stolen her last biscuit. I was kind of proud of her. All four bullies were well taken care of. We ran down the hill, picked up our baby sister from the sister and started to walk home. We walked through the housing projects, a place we wished we could live, but ma wouldn't leave that old sorry man of hers. Now we were heading home picking twigs and leaves out of our hair to a well-deserved ass whooping with a smile.

Some crimes were worth the punishment.

Time for a Change

Sister Sarah Ann and Sister Willie Bell were so intent on talking about Rose Lee, that they did not notice the small figure crouching in the shadow.

"Chile, you see them old runned over shoes? Lawdy-mercy, Rose Lee should be ah' shame of herself. Coming to church looking like a Goodwill reject." Sister Sarah Ann snickered. Sister Willie Bell, not to be outdone chimed in.

"Why don't she do something with all that wild hair on her head. Looking like she could get a pressing or something, always walking around with a nappy head. With a man like John Henry looks like she would try to keep herself up. That man is always casket sharp every Sunday. I love to see him walk, Sister Cat. He gives me sweats just looking at'im." They walked on down the hall and turned the corner. The little figure detached itself from the shadows.

"Uhuh, Talking about my ma I'll give you something to sweat about Old Heifas."

Scurrying quickly out the side door into the parking lot, the tiny figure darted to Sister Sarah Ann's new Cadillac. The one she liked to park on the crest of the hill, right where everyone coming to church could see it. The small hand tried the door handle, and it opened with a satisfying click. Shifting the gear stick into the reverse position, the little figure crouched in front of the pretty car's fender and gently rocked it. It started to slowly move on its own. Once it did the little figure darted back into the sanctuary, gave the Sunday school teacher a bright smile and hander her purse to her.

In a matter of minutes, one could hear a loud grinding sound then all hell broke loose. Crash! Boom! Crunch! Everybody ran out of the church to see what was going on. Sister Sarah's once fine Cadillac was crumbled at the bottom of the hill. It must have hit every car parked on the hillside as it fell. No one had a clue as to what happened or why. Rose Lee looked at her daughter and just knew.

Now sitting in her little green rocking chair in the corner, Gamin Jordan tried to see the small black and white tv. Her older brothers and siters laid spread out across the floor, on pillows and pallets. Every so often she could peek at her mother moving slowly around the house. Rose Lee was a stoutly built sturdy woman with calf muscles bigger than most people's thighs. For all of her sturdy stature she was a timid and meek spirit.

Work-worn and world-weary by hard times, she remained humble and gentle.

Gamin sat swinging her feet from side to side waiting for Ma to get through with cleaning so she could deal with her. She had already been marched home from church with her ear twisted, "Ma just don't understand them old Heifer's are evil." Gamin thought jumping slightly.

Hearing the sound of heavy footsteps on the porch the older children ran out of the room in fright. Gamin had been told to stay in her chair, and that's exactly what she did. Her thin arms folded across her chest, she knew it was the Ole Man and she was not moving.

Her mother went to open the door, but before she could reach it, the door flew open with a loud SHABOOM!

"John... wh... what's wrong?" she asked stammering, stepping back as he advanced into the room. The smell of alcohol and smoke preceded him into the room in a cloud. His presence filled the room menacingly. Ma tried to soothe the anger off his dark brow, but he just grabbed her wrist and backhanded her across the face.

Gamin knew he beat on her mom, everybody knew it. No one ever tried to help her get away from him though. She stood still not moving not taking her eyes off of them.

All the way home she was told when to fight and when to walk away. "Well now Ma, what's it gonna be fight or walk away." She wondered as her almond-colored eyes met those of her mom's. Ma wiped blood off her cheek looking at her baby sitting there watching her. Her hand curled into a tight fist, the ole man saw it and laughed in her face.

"What…" wheezing as he laughed. "Whatcha go do wit that, get yo self hurt." He laughed in Ma's face stepping up to her. A nerve in ma's jaw started twitching. Their eyes met again. Gamin sat up straight as she watched the change come over her mom. With wide eyes she knew she would remember this day for the rest of her life.

Ma drew back her fist and swung with all her might in an upward motion. Her fist collided with his chin. The look of shock and disbelief was priceless. The punch was so forceful that it sent him airborne, propelled him back out the door. The momentum carried him across the porch, and he landed on the concrete steps with a sickening crunch. Everyone came out of the house to find him laying there with blood running out his mouth.

Gamin ran to the steps and started jumping up and down shouting.

"Whoop his ass, Ma! Whoop his ass! How it feel Huh? Kick'em, Ma. Kick that bitch to sleep!" Her sister grabbed her from behind, pulled away from him with such force that her little feet went flying trying to kick him. Ma told someone to call the ambulance and the police. Of course, the boys scattered at the first sign of lights. The Ole Man laid there moaning and groaning. One of the EMT's told Ma that there was a chance his back was broken. She told them to take him on, and she would not be going with them.

She took Gamin by the hand and sat down on the old porch rocker. She puled her into her lap and hugged her close. Vicki and Gail came and sat down beside them. She looked at her girls. They were growing up to be fine young ladies, and she was proud of them. She also knew there was no going back. Her coppery skin marked by worry and abuse, she tried to explain to them that although it was a long time coming and long overdue, she did not have it in her to hurt anyone.

"Ya'll know I love ya'll and would never do nothing to hurt no one, but a soul can only take so much." She sighed deeply. She told them that he was not always like this. At first, he was a good hardworking man. She explained how hard times led him to being constantly locked up, just because some rich farmer wanted free laborers. Ma explained how these things could rob a man of his self-respect and his dignity. His drinking and whoring were a side effect of the poverty riddled life they were forced to live.

Gamin looked at her mom, shaking her little nappy head trying to get down, but her mom just pulled her closer. She stopped wiggling and looked at her mother for the first time to see tears running down her cheek. She tried to wipe them away. Her sisters got up and hugged their mom in a group hug.

"No Ma stop crying. It's okay, Ma. He was just bad. Ma, you went through too, and you didn't turn out bad. He was just plain mean from the start." Rose Lee's heart swelled as she made a promise to her girls that night. He's not coming back.

"We go be on our own from here on in. Until you girls find a good husband to care for you". She gave each of them a kiss on the forehead.

This was the first time of many more when the sisters would come together to cry, laugh, and pray their way through the troubles and trial of this cold world. Rose Lee knew that her girls were going to be alright as long as they had each other.

Journey's End

From the very first memory it was one of broken trust. The smell of a cow barn and the bubble of innocence burst.

As the violator's continued to violate all hope and faith quickly dwindles, like ashes in a windstorm. A small voice whispers into the night, "God if you are listening, please, oh please help me. Send someone, anyone to get me. The police, a preacher, a teacher, or just a friend. If you can't send me help or make them step at least show some mercy. Let me die tonight!"

The childish prayer whispered in the night went unanswered, but not unheard for the angel in Heaven wiped their teary eyes. They knew that her suffering would last many, many more sunrises. The prayers slowly stopped as shame and disgrace entered in. The little girl grew into a woman. Promiscuity is how she covered her sins. The sins were not her own. She had committed non. Her soul was dead, her conscious silent. Her childish prayer she would not admit.

"What's the use of prayer," she responded when asked. "There's non one to hear it. No one cared. My innocence was murdered. My stupid faith beat out of me destroying who I am. What's the use of spouting off words when nobody really gives a damn? She shook her childish head in anger. "What's the use of going to church? A house full of hypocrites. I've probably screwed them all, even the man in the pulpit."

Living the life, she learned from birth was all she knew how to do. She staggered along, stopping every now and then to have a fuck or two. Each time she made a stop it was like swallowing a bitter pill. She would get drunk or high again because the thought of it made her ill. Head aching, stomach sour, body smelling like strange man's sperm, she headed for a long hot shower, a couple of aspirin, was all she needed to be ready to go again.

Baby number one came along. It didn't stop a thing. After two and three confirmed to her a life of servitude was not how she wanted to live.

From the abuse of the past and the degrading of this last try, she knew in her heart salvation was a lie. Enters in number four and what do you know with this one was her last chance.

He knew what she was from the moment they met. She often reminded him of that."

I'm a whore from birth and I'll be one til I'm die. I would change if I could. I can't so why try." He heard what she said looking into her joy-defeated eyes. He could see the good and the fear she tried so hard to hide.

He would love her despite all she did to him. She didn't see what he knows her past was doing to them. He stood by her side in the time of needing someone the most he was there. She didn't want to see and know how much it cost.

All she knew was that he would never go away. Now she looked back along the way at all she had done. She questioned him with tears in her eyes, "Why did you stay?" With a smile on his face and understanding in his eyes he replied, "You have to dig through a lot of rock and garbage to find true love's diamond inside. I knew you the night we met, that we were meant to be this way."

It was the last time she asked that question. Her cold hart began to thaw. The healing had begun over aged old wounds that still felt fresh and raw. Hiding in his love she still sometimes wondered,

"Is this where the journey ends?"

Grandma's Table

There is a room in every home that houses the pulse of a family; that room where all family issues were handled and the fact of life taught. Seated around the old wooden table nothing was off limits. The women of the family were already seated around the table.

Kathleen, the oldest is standing by the backdoor, waving a pressing comb in front of a box fan to blow the smell of fresh pressed hair out of the room.

Charlene sat holding a spoon over her ear to keep from getting burned by the hot comb. Charlene's daughter is laughing at her cringing way every time the comb came near.

"Mom you should be used to getting a pressing by now. Aunt Kat can do some hair. Look at mine," she said shaking her head of thick silky freshly pressed shimmering hair. Charlene rolled her eyes at her daughter. Everyone in the room was laughing and talking. No one wanted to mention the one empty stool in the room. This was where the youngest in the group had always sat ever since the age of five when their mom sat her there. Every Saturday this is where she would sit until now. Kathleen's daughter tried to comfort her.

"Mom, it's gonna be okay. She will come around. It just gonna take a minute is all. She knows ya'll love her and Granny Greta did too." Farrah told her mother the missing family member had been her best friend since they were babies. She knew things would work out.

A loud silence fell over the kitchen as Dangee stood in the doorway. The expression on her face spoke volumes. Everyone's eyes fell to the crumpled obituary she held clinched in her fist. She walked into the room and place it on the table so that everyone could see it.

"Who is this?" she aske pointing to her name with the surviving offspring. Her eyes glued on the woman she had always known as mom.

"Baby, yo...!" Kathleen tried to explain, Dangee cut her off.

"I'm not your baby, just tell me who the hell am I?" The hurt in her voice was all but tangible.

"Come on in and sit down; Let's talk about this. "Charlene tried to hug her, but she jerked away from her. Mothers and daughters stood together to withstand the force of the hurt, betrayal, and bitter anger.

"Dangee, there is a good reason for this if you would let us explain." Kathleen spoke softly trying to ease the pain she hated to see. She slipped her arm around Dangee's shoulders and sat her down. Everyone else took their seat at the table as Kathleen began to tell her about her mother.

"Greta, our mother was going through the change of life when she got with you. We were all grown, living our own lives, raising our own kids. Carrying you took a toll on her health. The state had planned to take custody of you, but mom would have fought with her last breath. So, we all got together and decided that since I was the oldest, I would get custody of you.

Mom wanted you so bad that we did what we thought was best to keep you together. Mom knew it was going to come out, but she didn't' want to see you in this kind of pain, Baby believe me when I say If it was not for mom, we would have told you before now."

Walking across the kitchen Kathleen opened the china cabinet and took out a large leather-bound bible She laid it on the table in front of Dangee. There it was the recording of her birth in her mother's shaky hand, the time of her birth, the person who delivered her and where she was born. Smiling sadly, she caressed the handprint. A lone tear rolled down her pecan toned cheek. She could feel the anger receding the hurt, the hurt not so much. Looking at the bible assured her that she was loved.

Dangee sat back heavily, not knowing what to say or do. She looked up at her oldest sisters for guidance Everyone held her and promised her that they would always be there for her no matter what. Just like they had promised their mother they would. Everyone had a good cry and relaxed, laughing, and joking each other, as one after the other took a turn under the pressing comb. As if it was an after thought Dangee turned and asked no one in particular,

"Would anybody happened to know who my father was? So, mom got horny. She didn't get me by herself." No one answered because momma didn't tell that part. Dangee looked at each one of them and smiled,

"Oh well it doesn't matter, I got all I need in ya'll."

A Living Dream. A Short Story

The Dreams

"Oh, my goodness!" she moaned in aroused agony. Her nerves were screaming throughout her body for release. Fingers and toes spreading while flashes of white-hot heat took her breath away. A chill settled over her body as he stroked the lips of her womanhood. He slowly stroked his way up her body with moist kisses and nibbles. It made her bite her lip to keep from screaming. His large brown hands covered her breast caressing, kneading as he kissed a path from her navel to her chin. He whispered soft words of appreciation and encouragement.

Ti'Cara's heart was beating so hard and loud that it made her dizzy. She gripped and stoked the smooth dark shoulders, running her fingers around the cup of his ears begging him to move closer. Her sensitized breast was like bricks on her chest. Her womanhood was a soaking puddle between her ass cheeks. She threw her head back as his mouth closed on her neck, kissing, licking, and caressing. He took both of her wrist in one of his large hands pinning them over her head. Now they were face to face. She could taste his breath.

"Look at me!" He demanded in a harsh whisper. "Look at me, I want you to see me when I take you." She slowly opened her eyes only to get lost in the darkest brown eyes she had ever seen. She lay there, hot, and molten arching her body straining to get closer to the heat that was him. "Now Derek! Now!" She silently screamed to him through clenched teeth. He obliged and joined their bodies together. His deep animal like growl mixed with hers. He silenced them both with a dep soul bending kiss. Explosions of light, colors and sound engulfed them as they wrestled and strained to become one.

Ti'Cara sat up in her bed drenched in sweat, touching her body. It was wet and throbbing. Looking around wildly she threw back the covers and ran for the shower. "What fool would be in the shower at three in the fucking morning?" She snapped in disgust at herself. The answer to her question was across town at the Northern Lights Inn and Suites.

Across town, Derek Cumpton was having a rough night. It was the same dream and the same female pixie. She would pour herself all over him like caramel syrup.

Lord her body was a small wonderland of excitement and pleasure. This time was different, he could see her face. She was a delight to behold. Even under the stinging cold spray of water his body hardened just thinking about her husky cries of pleasure at his touch. "Damn it!" He growled as he began to handle his problem the old fashion way.

Northern Light's Poolside

Derek didn't intend to eavesdrop on the woman's conversation, but the self-disgust in one of their voices stopped him in his tracks and the outright humor in the other made him smile to himself. He listened in on the Home Girl conversation. What he heard next put a frown on his smooth brown skin.

"Kayla, stop it! You idiot! This is not funny. I've had to deal with this X-rated dream for a week now. I can't sleep. Stop laughing at me." Ti'Cara snapped in frustration making Kayla laugh even harder.

"Kayla! I can't sleep, eat, or even take a freaking shower without him being there. I even spoke his name. I saw his face; I could even taste his breathe. God, I'm going crazy." She continued to whine in a quiet desperation in her voice. Kayla finally stopped laughing.

"Did you recognize him? Have you met him before? What does he look like?" Sitting on the lounger she had been reclining on. Ti'Cara turned to face her lifelong friend lowering her voice to speak. Derek had to lean against the door frame to hear even, stepping out of the room into the breezeway. What he heard was an edited version of his nighttime drama. Her deep sigh was so familiar his heart lurched while his loins tightened.

"I don't know anyone named Derek or anyone that looks like that. I mean, he's big, real tall, well over six feet, built like the Jolly Green Giant, real solid, milk chocolate skin that makes you want to lick it. He has these dark almost black eyes, and a well-trimmed mustache and beard. Oo chile his muscles, the brother is fine."

"It's scaring the hell out of me because I don't know where this is all coming from. I just want it to stop." She whispered in total surrender falling back onto the lounge chair. Kayla sat looking at her defeated friend not wanting to tell her that her dreams were just her emotions telling her it's time to live. It was time to love again.

"Well Baby Girl, I don't know what to tell you. I know if it was me, I'd just enjoy the hell out of my dreams, but you ain't me. I think you just need to get your fuck-on every now and then. Maybe you wouldn't be having these dreams." Kayla told her honestly trying to find an easy way to tell her that she was healed and ready for love again. Ti'Cara would crawl deeper into her shell if she just blurted that at her. She hated to see her withdraw from everyone, but for the life of her she didn't get why having a dram of good fucking scared the hell out of her.

"Kayla not everybody is dick happy like you. I'm just more selective than you are that's all." Ti'Cara said looking down at her pink toenails.

"Selective! Selective? You haven't had a dick in over five fucking years, and you know it. You just plain scared of men. You let that bastard handicap you. I know he's dead and buried, thank the Lord, but you're still letting him bully you. All men ain't like him. Shit, if you had told me half the shit, he did to you I would have killed the motherfucker myself." Kyla said as she got angry just thinking about what Eddie Burnbury had put her friend through. No woman deserved to be treated the way he treated Ti'Cara. His death was a blessing, accident or not. He deserved everything that he got if not more.

Derek stood listening, transfixed in place. He had a Chamber and Commerce meeting in town in an hour, but there was no way he was going to miss the chance to meet this young woman. He rescheduled his meeting for the next day. He hurriedly changed into swim trunks with sweats over them. While he dressed, he wondered would she look like the woman in his dream. Caramel-skin, full pouty lips, dark brown eyes, soft shoulder length dark brown hair. Would she have a cute girlish shape with small breast and a tiny waist with a slight flare at the hips. What his brother would call a pocket Venus. Small enough to put in your pocket, but big enough to love. He threw his beach towel over his shoulder and walked at naturally as he could to the pool area.

He was glad to see the women were still there. But which one was Cara? He listened to them as he casually walked behind them.

"Cara, if I were you and I ran a cross a brother that looked like that it would be on, all day fuckfest." Kyla said giggling. Cara couldn't help but laugh at her friend's silly antics. Then the thought hit her,

"You know, you're right that's just want I'm going to do. If I ever meet him, I'm not going to run away. This is one dream that will come true." She told Kayla. She immediately had a second thought and frowned,

"What if it's … you know…well, not like the

dream." Cara didn't have much experience with sex, so it was a good question. Kayla laughed. and replied,

"Then you make it better than the dream. Believe me you need no instructions, listen to your body, and follow through. It's not like you're looking for lover or nothing, just a good time. Think of it as therapy. It can help you get over your fears." Kayla advised while Cara shook her head.

"You are a serious nut case, but it kind of makes sense. I might just try that..." Cara's words cut off as she stared straight at the pool gate. Kayla could hear them opening. She looked around and gasped. Cara was frozen, her mouth moving like a fish as her eyes followed the man as he dropped his towel ad pulled off his sweats.

Derek positioned himself at the far end of the pool. He knew which woman was Cara the minute he laid eyes on the two women. His eyes ra over her slim frame. His heart was beating so hard he was amazed no one could see his chest moving. Another part of his body recognized him too. Feeling his dick hardening he hurriedly finish taking off his sweats, and shades and dived into the pool.

Cara was frozen her eyes riveted to the man gliding through the water. They followed the way his body moved, his muscles flexing with each stroke. Her breathing increased, her ears were ringing, and speaking was out of the question. Kayla looked from her little friend to the fine brother that was gliding through the water. She was aware of him the moment he entered the courtyard. She was also aware of him checking them out as he made his way around the pool. She smiled to herself, "This is going to be interesting."

"Cara, I've got to go check on our new intern. She's smart but I gotta make she she'd on point.," Kayla said patting Cara's hand and eased out of the courtyard. She hurried to her office and keyed up the poolside camera, then sat back and watched.

Cara didn't realize Kayla was gone. She was too immersed in the figure in the pool. Her heart was thumping like a caged bird against her ribs. Her breath was burning her lungs and her nipples had hardened. She couldn't take her eyes off of him. Mesmerized at his movements, muscles bouncing up and relaxing as he got out of the pool his body glistening as he dried off.

Cara was transfixed her eyes were absorbing

the sight of him. They traveled up and down his torso then moved farther down. The sight made her jump. She snapped out of her lust induced daze. Her eyes met his. He gave her a half smile and headed her way. He kept his towel hanging over his shoulder to cover his bulging front, Cara looked around wildly.

"Oh, my goodness, oh my goodness." She scrambled around gathering her things so she could make a run for it. Too late! His shadow covered her making her raise her head. The visual she had from her position made her throat and mouth dry up forcing her to swallow. Her eyes drinking in thick calf muscles, well defined thighs to the apex of his manhood. She had no idea how long she stared at the thin material covering him. Her eyes followed the thin trail of hair that widened as it traveled up his chest. She knew it must feel soft as down feathers. His shoulders looked massive. The muscles in his necked moved up and down. She knew how it tasted. His lips soft but strong jawline jutted out to create a totally handsome face, as their eyes met Cara knew she was gone.

The sexual tension was almost tangible. Derek had never experienced anything this strong in his life. Something in him was screaming run the other way, but the hunger for this female was much too great. He couldn't turn away even if his life depended on it. No words were spoken so they joined hands and went to the poolside sitting area.

Trying to ease her unspoken fears, Derek knew he had to move slow. Not too slow is body screamed at him. "Hello love, my name is Derek Cumpton Tell me about your dreams and I'll tell you mine. Is that fair enough. We're not strangers. In our dreams we know each other in the most intimae way. There should be no secrets even in our dreams." He spoke softly comforting so not to scare her off. To Ticara he could have asked her anything in that voice it was done. Her eyes never leaving his lips her body remembering how they felt moving over her skin.

Nervously she started to tell him, stuttering and blushing. She had to lick her lips repeatedly. Internal heat was drying her mouth. Derek realized his mistake each time she licked her lips his manhood got harder and hotter. Thank God for his sweats.

"Ti'Cara, stop please. You don't know what you're doing to me." He whispered harshly the softness gone, replaced with a painful hunger. At first his tone confused her then understanding dawned she smiled a wicked smile.

"Stop what? This" She teased as she ran her tongue over her soft lips leaving them glistening. He almost lost it. She recognized the expression she had seen it when he demanded that she look at him. Not knowing what came over her, she continued to tease and taunt him.

"You know what you're doing and there is only so much I can take with you. Keep it up and you'll find out if reality lives up to the dream." He warned her. She laughed at him and stood up.

"Don't dare me, you may be the one that gets more than you asked for." She snapped back saucily. Derek stood up to see how far she would take this.

"210 my room. First one there gets to choose." He loved the way she tilted her head when she was thinking."

"Choose what?" she asked already knowing the answer.

"Top or bottom," He answered.

Catching him off guard she ran towards his room laughing. The sound floating back to him as he ran after her. When he caught up with her, she was opening his door. He knew he had locked it. It really didn't matter. He followed her inside.

She had started undressing, he stopped her by touching her hands that were on her zipper.

"let me." He sat on the foot of the bed tugging her to stand between his knees. He slowly undressed her kissing each inch of her flesh as he exposed it. Down one leg and up the other. Ticara was lightheaded by the time he made it back to her waist.

"This is what it feels like to swoon." She thought to herself with a giggle. He removed her little Victoria's Secret panties and buried her face in her curly black hairs. His tongue sweeping to divide her lips. Ticara's knees started to buckle. He held her around her waist to keep her upright while he made a meal of her.

She closed her eyes only to quickly open them again. The lights and colors were too intense. Taking a deep breath, she was determined to take control of this situation. Stepping back, she pushed him back on the bed. "My turn." She said her voice husky with arousal. Getting down on her knees she started at his ankles and kissed her way up his long, long legs. By the time she made it to his thighs his manhood stood out thick and throbbing. She kissed its base, the hairs tickling her nose before she could make it to the head strong hands griped her shoulders and pulled her up his long body. In her mind she compared him to a tall chocolate mountain and God knows she loved herself some chocolate.

She began to kiss, lick, and nibble any piece of flesh she could encounter. The chocolate mountain grunted and groaned like an awakening volcano with a secret. She wondered what it would take to make it explode.

Derek was throbbing. He couldn't hold back much longer, this little woman was turning him inside out, hands and mouth moving all over in every direction over his body. How many hands did she have? And those lips were amazing. He held her close and rolled over pinning her to the bed. "My turn." He mimicked her. He rained kisses all over her face, nibbled her neck then moved lower. When he frenched kissed her curly mounds, she screamed his name and tried to scoot back away from his onslaught. He laughed against her mounds at her maneuver.

"Oh no sweetness, no retreat. I just got started." He whispered and continued his attack. She could not move. He held her waist one hand above her pelvic and the other gripped her side. Ticara bit into a pillow to keep from screaming again. She had never felt like this colorful light danced behind her closed lids sweat ran down her face as she twisted and thrashed about. It was just as she had done in her dream. She reached down caressing his head, her fingers found his ears and circled them. Gently she tugged upward.

He followed stopping here and there to place a kiss or a nibble. He covered her completely using his knee he parted her thighs even wider so that he could settle his larger frame between her legs. His dick nudges her pussy opening the wet tightness that made him hesitate. Unsure was a new feeling for him, so he kissed her deeply. Her small hands fluttered on his shoulder looking down in her face he smiled to himself. "Nahh, you won't get off that easy." Gripping both of her hands he raised them above her head pinning them there with one of his.

"Look at me, open your eyes Ticara. I want you to see me when I take you." He demanded.

Her eyes fluttered open. Light brown met liquid chocolate. She licked her lips nervously. Arousal overcame fear. "Now Derek," her husky whisper sent him over the edge. Control completely gone. "Yes, now Ticara yes." He groaned deeply as he pushed into her tight wetness. Watching her face closely for any sign of discomfort. Biting down on her bottom lip as her eyes widen. He slowly moved in and out of her. With each stroke he went deeper giving her more and more of him, sweat ran down his face as he strained to keep from plunging into her tightness.

Cara felt like she was slowly being split open. He was too big, way too gig. She bit back a groan as she felt him go even deeper breathing deeply, she couldn't hold in the tortured sobs. Catching her breath as he stroked even deeper biting down on her lip, she forced her body to relax. "That's right baby relax I want to give you all of me. That's it breath, that's it." He spoke softly encouraging her. He could feel her small body open more giving him deeper access.

Telling himself to keep it slow he felt her hands grip his ass. Not realizing what she was up to until it was too late. He felt her hips move and then he was buried deep in her tight, oh so tight body to the hilt. She let out a loud agonizing groan. He froze. His dick was completely buried inside of her. He could feel the very end of her hot tight so sweet pussy.

Looking down at her face he expected to see pain. What he saw was pure rapture on her beautiful face. He kissed her grinding and stroking until they were screaming and clawing at each other like animals. He couldn't believe she took all of him. He didn't have to hold back. He felt her muscles squeeze his dick until he knew he couldn't hold his nut nay longer his big body jerked violently as he unloaded.

Cara felt him jerk inside of her. Her pussy responded hips grinding and pumping against him throwing her into a windstorm. "Derek help me." She screamed as the orgasm gripped her. Fear like none she had ever known closed around her. She struggled for breath. Derek hearing her panic held her close.

"I got ya babe, just hold on, hold on." He whispered in her ear as they both gave in to the power of their climax. Together they flew to the stars on tidal waves of release. He rolled over and fear gripped him. He knew things had gotten a little rough, hurting her was the last thing he wanted to do, looking down at her face he watched tears run down the side of her face. From the corner of her eyes. His heart missed a beat,

"Ticara, baby, are you alright? Please… I didn't… did I hurt you?" he asked kissing her tears gently. "I'm sorry baby, forgive me." He whispered sincerely mentally urging her to look at him. She exhaled heavily her eyes opened as a tiny smile touched her swollen lips. Light brown eyes searched his face with a questioning gave in them.

"I'm fine. Yes, it hurt. Don't be sorry. I knew it was going to hurt before we started. I wouldn't have traded tis for anything. I've never did that before it was worth the pain'. She told him trying to explain how he made her feel.

Derek watched her face as she spoke looking for what he didn't know. What he did know was that he would never forget her beautiful face at this moment. Caressing her face gently he knew he was a goner. Love had trapped him at last. "TiCara are you sure? I would never intentionally hurt you." He spoke softly placing a kiss on her temple. She was quite for a while. Then she looked at him.

"You cheated." She told him softly playing

with the soft hairs on his chest.

"Cheated... What do you mean?" He asked lost for a second. He watched that that same wicked smile touches her lips.

"I won." She said on a yarn leaning her head on his shoulder. Her lashes floated down. He knew she was tired because he was too.

"You won the race, ahh next time." He smiled placing a kiss on her forehead thinking ahead to their next time. Sleep claimed them both while his arm curved protectively around her. Nothing he promised himself, nothing was going to come between them.

The Meeting

Kayla sat in the office as the action at the pool took place. She watched Cara's instinct to run and let out a sigh of relief when Derek cornered her. She gave him a thumbs up. "Get that girl." She silently encouraged. She laughed at the expression on Cara's face as she took in the offering in front of her. She looked like a woman in shock.

Kayla couldn't help but laugh, they both had comical expressions on their faces. She had to admit the boy was fine. Tall with seriously well-defined muscles. From the way those trunks fit, boy was packing some serious meat. With that thought she did start to worry about Cara. If anybody deserved to get their fuck on it was her, but dude was a heavy weight. He towered over her, the top of her heard barely reached the middle of his chest. His arm was thick as Cara's little thighs.

On the screen they were sitting at the poolside courtyard. Cara was talking and there was a subtle change in her posture. She went from cowering to teasing with the toss of her head. Kayla's fingers flew across the keyboard as she tried to boost the volume. She wanted to know what Cara was saying to put a shocked look on the Green Giant's face.

"...more than you asked for." Kayla let out a shocked squeal as Cara stood up to face the Giant across the table. "210, my room. First one there gets to choose." His deep voice came across the speaker. The tilt of Cara's head told Kayla what the answer was going to be. She sat back in her chair as the two ran for the hotel room. Kayla turned the camera on the door to 210. As she got caught up in her paperwork. She prayed that her little friend would handle her business and back up the challenge she issued.

Cara yawned and stretched widely arching her back like a cat. She winched as pain shot through her pelvic to her navel making her gasp sharply. "Damn another dream." She mumbled rolling out of bed only to realize she was naked. A frown settled on her brow as she touched her naked breast. They were tender. Slowly she touched he pussy. It was swollen. She sat up looking around wildly. "I can't believe I did this. Oh, my goodness. What the hell!" she started to get up but jumped and screamed at a noise behind her.

"It's a little late to cover up don't you think," Derek's deep voice came from the bathroom door. Dressed in nothing but boxers his wide chest bare.

"I um... I do... I don't know what to say. I'm...I'm not like this. I don't sleep around." She stammered and stuttered embarrassed and a little confused. Derek pushed off of the door frame unfolding his arms. He walked down to the bed. Cara tensed up. The look of panic was replaced with shame.

Derek didn't understand it. What they shared was too beautiful and mind blowing he refused to let her spoil it with guilt.

"TiCara I know that. Only a fool could think otherwise. Come here. Let's soak in the tub. It will help ease the soreness." He didn't give her a chance to say anything, swooping down he picked her up and carried her to the bathroom. She started to resist then thought better of it. The warm water was heaven to her sore muscles. Derek sat behind her messaging her back, and neck. Ticara was in another world his magic hands went to work on her.

"Tell me about it. I want to know who hurt you." It was a request in that soft sensitive voice that Ticara couldn't resist. She hesitated a few minutes then slowly began telling him the story of her life.

Her parents died in a tornado when she was

two years old. She would have died too if it hadn't been for a firefighter who heard her cry. Her grandparents had taken her in. She was a very sheltered child, overprotected, and a basically good kid. She was an overachiever even by today's standards, and graduated college at the age of nineteen with her doctorates. Her graduation had been tarnished. She hated to even think about it. She had lost the only family she had that day. They had been on their way to her graduation when a semi ran a red light killing them instantly. She remembered how Kayla had sheltered her afterwards.

She remembered so many people where at her house the next day. There was Eddie Brackton, who had made himself indispensable. He and Kayla had had a big fight and she left the house. She couldn't remember everything that happened. She just recalled a couple of months later she was married to Eddie Burnbury. If she thought she was going through hell with the death of her grandparents, her marriage to Eddie had been a train wreck.

After the I do's, the abuse started with him yelling and calling her names. Her wedding night was only the tip of the iceberg. He would beat her for anything, for nothing at all. Even the sex was violent. It was so violent that now she realized that it was rape from the beginning. He would choke her until she passed out.

He started brining home sex toys to use on her and use them he did. He'd always been mean. Even on their wedding night she didn't understand what all the sex talk was about. With Eddie she always felt empty and abused. There was no good feeling at all. None of the things she'd heard about making love ever happened to her. She learned to fake it as she grew numb to his taunts and abuse.

Then one night all through dinner he bragged about how he was going to put it on her. He was going to make her beg him to stop. She was going to feel him this time. He had taken a pill that someone had sold him. It was supposed to keep him hard longer. The more he talked the more he drank. The bottle of vodka was almost empty,

She didn't respond to any of his taunts. She busied herself with cleaning up the kitchen. She was loading the dishwasher when he came up behind her. She knew her time was up. He grabbed her by the hair and drug her up the stairs. She tried to fight back, but he only laughed at her and got more excited. Before the night was over, she would be fighting for her very life. He had come to her like a rabid animal. He ripped her clothes off and throwed her around like a ragdoll. He laid her over the foot of the bed and rammed her so hard she gasped for air.

"I bet you felt that! Big Daddy's gonna beat that pussy up tonight." He screamed at her holding her face against the bed his hand pressed hard against her neck. She lost count of how long or how many times he got at her. She did scream. She did cry and beg him to stop. That only made him get worse. The last thing she remembered was him twisting her arms behind her pouring hot oil down the crack of her as. He had gripped her ass and rammed into her with so much force her teeth clacked together.

The pain was awful, and she screamed again and again. She remembered him pulling out of her and mumbling. When she heard the nightstand, drawer open she knew what he was getting. He had brought home this monster of a dick thick black and twelve inches long. More than two inches around. He strapped it on. She tried to get away from him. But he grabbed her.

First, he fucked the pussy trying to force all of it in her. She felt something inside her tear loose. Blood covered the dick and he shouted for joy. The pain was blinding. Praying that he would stop, too weak to fight back he threw her over the tub and shoved it up her asshole. She screamed until she lost all rational thought. Freed by darkness that closed in around her for the last time. What all he did to her after that she didn't know.

Hours later she woke up in an ambulance. The sirens ringing in her head, her body was o fire. She flayed around only to be restrained by the MT. She could hear voices but couldn't see anyone. Was she dead? Did she go to hell? All of her life she had strived to be good, respected her parents, and her elders, did excellent in school, never harmed another living creature and she still ended up in hell. Tears burned her eyes as darkness saved her again.

Opening her eyes two weeks later, Ticara's eyes met worried dark brown eyes of her best friend Nykayla. She lifted her hand trying to speak. Kayla had stopped her telling her, she had taken care of everything. Everything meant burying Eddie who died in a car wreck that same night he had tried to kill her. She had signed release papers for the five surgeries she had to undergo to save her life. All the while posing as her sister Kayla took care of her little friend the best she could.

She didn't have anyone else. She didn't tell her about Eddie until a week later. Ticara refused to go back to the house. Kayla had Eddie's house torn down and the lot grazed over as if no one ever had been there.

Ticara had been bullied into going to counseling and to start handling her family business. It had been over five years since she had thought about it or talked to anyone except Kayla and her counselor. She spoke matter of factly about it. Derek knew that years of Counseling and the love of Kayla had brought her this far. Her face was void of any emotion as she spoke about it. She told him how terrified of men she had been. No man had touched her in all that time.

That is not until he invaded her dreams. Her body had recognized him. Derek would have done anything to take that dead look out of her eyes and off of her face. He reached for her and hugged her close to him wanting to shield her from those horrific memories. Holding her with one arm he grabbed one of the hotel bath sheets and wrapped her in it. Lying her on the bed her rubbed her dry. She purred like a lazy kitten.

Derek enjoyed it as much as she did. She looked at him and smiled. "It's next time." She whispered. Derek laughed at her. "Oh yeah, man burn the black book," he thought to himself. His parents had always told him when true love showed up, grab it with both hands. Don't let go. He would know it when it came his way. He did!

In Love

Hunger got them out of bed finally a couple of hours later. There were a lot of fancy places to eat, but Ticara liked the atmosphere of Helen's Kitchen, a casual family restaurant, so that's where they went. It was late when they got back. Derek had an early meeting the next day and Ticara didn't want him to miss it. She kissed him at his door and smiled.

"Thank you, Derek. I'll see you in my dreams." She told him with wanting in her voice. He started to unlock his door when a thought struck him.

"Hey, Ticara, how did you get in my room this morning?" He asked puzzled. She started laughing at him.

"I own the inn." She told him. Sweetly watching his jaw drop in surprise she walked away laughing.

Kayla had left a note telling Ticara to give her a call. Ticara decided not to. She wanted to hold what she had found close to her heart just a little while longer. It was about ten o'clock in the morning when she made it home. It didn't surprise her to see Kayla's car outside or that she was in her house waiting on her. "Oh well time to face the firing squad." Ticara thought to herself as she walked in the door.

Kayla had been so worried she couldn't stay away. She had to make sure her little friend was okay. She knew firsthand what her friend had been through. She's the one who found her that morning. Whenever she thought about Eddie Brackton, she would see her friend's broken body on the bathroom floor. The smell had stayed with her for months. She had called a cleaning service to clean the house. She didn't want Ticara to return to the sight of her torture the way it was. It really didn't make a difference because she refused to go back there.

Ticara gave away everything including her clothing. After leaving the hospital she moved back to her grandparents' house. She had Eddie's big house burned down and the lot grazed. Kayla took over running the inn and had later told Cara that the inn had been left to her. Ticara also owned an apartment complex and three restaurants. Kayla forced her to handle her business and to stand on her own two feet but let her know she would always be there if she needed her.

To think she had encouraged her to screw that giant. Ain't no telling what he would do to her. Kayla heard the car pull up in the drive and started for the door just as Cara walked in singing softly. Kayla folded her arms mimicking her mother before Cara could say any thing Kayla tore into her.

"Just what were you thinking hiding in room 210 all dang day? You could have called me, texted me, hell... I would have settled for a smoke signal. How could you let me worry about you like this? I've been going out of my mind thinking of you and the Jolly Bro Giant. I had to be physically restrained from coming to that room. I was afraid he was doing Lord knows what to you. That you might have needed me. I let you down again." She was almost screaming now in frustration.

Cara let her get it all out. The tears in her hard as nails friend's eyes tore at her heart. She hurried over to her and hugged her close.

"It's alright Kay, I'm fine. I was well taken care of and it was awesome." She held her by her elbows looking up in her friend's eyes grinning broadly. Cara was only five feet two and a half inches. Whereas Kayla was five ten. The height difference made them an odd couple to see. It suited them, big sister, and little sister.

Kayla sighed heavily. The happiness on Cara's face was worth the worry. "Awesome! It was awesome? Come on baby tell momma everything. If that man did anything perverted to you, I'll make him regret it the day he was born." She warned.

Cara giggled. The rest of the night was taken up with girl talk and a bottle of Moscato. They talked and giggled until the sun had started to rise. Kayla was satisfied that Derek sounded pretty decent. But she would make sure when she got to the office.

Derek and TiCara spent every free minute together for the next two weeks. Derek had to go back home to attend his business. His brother Teague was holding things down while he was scouting out places in Mississippi to develop.

C&C Developers was looking to expand into Mississippi. Kayla and Cara showed him two prime tracks that would be perfect. When he asked about the owner of the first property Kayla point to Cara. The second larger track belonged to Kayla. Derek had to laugh at them. They were a pair of quick witted bopsy twins. He couldn't wait for Teague to meet Kayla, upbeat, outspoken, outgoing, in your face. She was a firecracker. Poor Teague. He won't know what hit him.

In two weeks of their poolside meeting Derek had the opportunity to observe the two in different settings. TiCara was more reserve in her taste of dress. Kayla was the total opposite. For a tall lady she wore everything with a certain panache that one couldn't help but notice.

Ticara drove him to the airport. She was silent the entire trip. "Was she upset about something?" Derek thought to himself. They had an hour's wait at the airport. Derek took that time to find out what was bugging his little lady. She didn't want him to go. She would miss him too much. It was going to hurt. He hugged her close to him telling her he would be back in a week or two. He went on to say, they would talk on the phone every night at a quarter past nine and not to worry.

Ticara wiped tears from her eyes as the big plane shot down the runway. This is going to be the longest two weeks ever. The first week TiCara moped around until Kayla couldn't take it any longer. Always the mother hen, she gave her a good talking to then bullied her into handling her business. In her office TiCara did get busy. She went over financial reports from the townhouses and the restaurants. Everything was in the black showing excellent profits. She ordered two knew grills and ovens and ordered an upgrade on all of her walk-in refrigerators for the restaurant. It kept her busy during the day. It was the nighttime that stirred her up. At home she would relax with a glass of wine or a shot of bourbon and think of Derek.

Derek worked like a maniac. He came in early and left late. Teague was watching his normally laid-back brother work like a possessed workaholic. He even worked on the weekend. After church Teague cornered him.

"What gives Li'l D. You acting strange since your trip. The tracks of land are exactly what we were looking for. Dad was impressed with the estimates you calculated. You didn't go out this weekend and I haven't seen any of your lay-n-waits around." That's what they called Derek's lady friends. Teague continued, "No late lunches. Come on man give up the dirt." Teague crossed his arms over his massive chest. Being the oldest brother had its advantages. He outweighed Derek by twenty-five pounds didn't hurt either.

Teague didn't know what was bugging Derek, but what he heard wasn't what he expected. In love, his baby brother was in love. He couldn't wait to tell their mother and father. On the way home Teague called his parents. His mom was excited, and father was amused. Teague wanted to know more about this Ticara Hamilton.

Nykayla sat at her desk wondering what to do. The report she had gotten back on Derek. He was well educated and a hard worker. No criminal background. Business wise he was respected and well spoken of in the business world. He was one of the most eligible bachelors in two counties in Florida. He had a lot of close calls with false paternity suites. That made him more selective about the women he associated with. No current attachments in the last six months.

Teague was eyeing his report on TiCara Carmel Hamilton. Raised by elderly grandparents, graduated top of her class in high school and college. Lost grandparents on their way to her graduation. Married Eddie Brackton three months later, who was later found dead in a car wreck. One year later heart attack with a question mark.

She was in the hospital some speculated that she had something to do with it. She didn't attend the funeral. She later took over the running of the family business and was a very profitable woman with a net worth of a couple of million dollars easy. Teague didn't know how to approach Derek with the question mark knowing how he felt about his angel. Teague knew it was going to be hard, but he had to tell him somehow.

Derek was inpatient. The plane wasn't flying fast enough for him. He was headed back to TiCara. His heart was beating so hard he was going to be with her again. Holding her again. She was meeting both he and Teague at the airport. Teague insisted on coming. Derek didn't put up a fight he didn't care if the whole family came as long as he got to see TiCara.

Teague had seen pictures of TiCara, but to see her in person was different. As they walked into the airport, he saw this pint-sized woman dressed in nice fitting jeans and pink t-shirt. On her feet were pink and white New Balance sneakers. Carmel skinned; a beautiful face surrounded by a pixie haircut. He studied her as she ran towards them. Derek dropped his bags and met her halfway. She jumped into his arms.

Derek held her tight kissing her passionately. Yep, his little brother was a goner. He picked up Derek's bags and went to join the happy couple. Standing beside them made him realize just how delicate she really was. She barely came up to his chest. Derek introduced them. Teague like her voice, soft and melodious. She had a shy bewitching smile and a cute little shape. The girl had the right stuff. They were making small talk when someone behind them cleared their throat loudly. All three turned at the same time towards the sound.

Teague's breath was trapped in his throat at the young woman behind them. TiCara laughed as Derek hugged her friend. Kayla was dressed like Kayla dresses. She had on a Baby Phat blue jean mini skirt exposing a mile or two of legs and matching half jacket that left her midriff out. In her navel was a diamond belly ring. She topped it all off with five-inch heels.

Teague's eyes travelled up long well shaped legs to the teasing twinkle of her belly ring, on up to nice rounded thirty-eight c's barely concealed by the jacket, on to her ruby red lips. Green amused eyes clashed with chocolate brown. It was a challenge. Introductions were made and Kayla naturally took over. Teague was awestruck. Leading them out to the parking lot Kayla strutted. Teague's eyes closely followed the movement of her rounded ass as it bounced around under her barely there skirt. The curve in her back and flatness of her stomach made him want to see how well she would fit in the crook of his arm. He couldn't believe he was getting excited just watching her walk. It was a hell of a walk though.

Derek rode with TiCara, Teague rode with Kayla to the inn and got him checked in. Ticara laid her head back against the headrest. Looking at him from the corner of her eyes she smiled. "I've missed you so much these last two weeks. I did get a lot of work done though." She laughed. Derek laughed also.

"I think I did at least a month's worth of work. My family thinks something is wrong with me. That's way Teague is here. He just and to meet the woman that has me working so hard to get back to her." Derek laughed shaking his head. Ticara laughed with him.

"What would you like to do first?" She asked keeping her eyes on the road. Derek looked at her for a moment as if in deep thought He slid his hands across her thighs then down to her crotch. He applied enough pressure to make her body stiffen, and her breathing change. "Derek! Don't do that I'm driving." She tried to move his hand from between her legs. She started to get wet. Her feminine muscles tightening and released causing her to try to close her thighs. This she couldn't do and drive. He leaned close to her.

"What do you feel like doing first?" he whispered softly in her ear as he continued to message and tease her through her jeans. TiCara's eyes started to glaze over with heat. She shook her head and swallowed loudly.

"Stay on your side for five minutes, just five minutes then I'll show you what I feel like doing." She promised him through clenched teeth. Derek laughed softly and sat back in is seat. He was fascinated with beads of sweat that ran down her forehead down her jaw to her neck. He had to struggle with himself not to lean over and lick that busy little droplet off of her. He heaved and sighed.

"Five minutes is taking too long." He grunted at her. He could see the beginning of her wicked little smile that he had grown to love.

"Baby you don't know how much I've missed you. God, I didn't know I could miss someone so much." He told her holding her free hand tightly until she pulled into her garage. Before the door closed down Ticara was all over him. She rained kisses all over his face. Her tongue played around his ears. Her hips grinded and squeezed him. She pushed a button on the side of his seat that reclined the seat. Hands busy she hurriedly unzipped his slacks. Sitting on his lap she shimmed out of her jeans and underwear.

Derek folded his arms behind his head surrendering to her sweet torture. He almost jumped out of the seat when her small hands grabbed his engorged manhood in a strangle hold. All he could do was grab the headrest and hold on. TiCara was intent on releasing all of her pint up needs starting now. She kissed the thick base licking the thick throbbing vein that fed his need. She loved the taste of him as she greedily moved upward squeezing him with both hands until she found his throbbing head which she took in her mouth. Tasting, sucking, playing with the opening with her tongue. Derek was about to lose it big time. What the hell was she doing to him, her mouth, lips, and hands were doing amazingly crazy things to him.

Not able to handle much more of her torture he pulled her up, his dick plopping out of her mouth. He impaled her on his pussy starved dick. TiCara screamed as he forced his way in her. Eyes wide with shock she tried to move away. He grabbed her waist and began to pump slowly in and out of her until he could feel her relax and open up for him.

He was afraid he had hurt or frightened her when he had taken her. The tightness of her had made him freeze for a moment, but it felt too good to stop. He forced himself to slow down. Finding her rhythm TiCara braced her hands on the roof of the car as she began to ride him. Derek lost it completely all he could do was feel. The intensity of their coupling burned hot and fast reaching their orgasm simultaneously they exploded calling each other's names holding on to each other until the tremors passed.

Slowly they made their way into the house stopping in each room to make love again and again. In the kitchen Derek lifted her up on the countertop and made a meal of her sending her to the brink of insanity again. TiCara got him in the living room pushing him over the back of her sofa.

She sucked, licked, and stroked his dick until he exploded in her mouth while calling her momma. She wiped her lips and giggled at him. He shook his head.

"I know I'll never hear the end of that one, but you can't have a momma without Big Daddy." He threatened snatching her up he headed for the bedroom where they would remain the rest of the evening, loving sleeping, and eating.

Big Bro, Lil Bro

Nykayla eyed the big, tall brother making himself comfortable in the passenger seat of her Expedition. He fumbled around the bottom of the seat searching for the recline button. She took pity on him opening the console she pressed the adjust button. The seat slid back to a more comfortable position. Her eyes followed his long legs as he stretched them out, all the way down to his size fourteen shoes. "This is one big ass brother." She thought as her eyes landed on his zipper. The thought struck her, "You know what they say about big feet." She dipped her head and giggled.

Teague cleared his throat loudly, and Nykayla looked up guiltily meeting his amused stare. Raising her eyebrows innocently she shrugged her shoulders. Her bare breast bouncing under the jacket.

"Hey, okay you can't blame a girl for wondering." She said with a gremlin grin. He shook his head and laughed, and she joined in. "Oh, you won't see Derek until later this evening or tomorrow. With the two of them you never know." She advised him shaking her head, he frowned at that.

"Okay, I won't worry, but where did he go?" Thinking the answer and wishing he was going in the same direction with this long-legged firecracker.

"Her place most likely. All of this is new for Cara. Going two weeks without seeing Derek was hard for her." Nykayla spoke matter-of-factly with a shrug of her shoulder. Teague searched her face for signs of deceit and found none. What he did see was a touch of worry. He gave her hand a slight squeeze. She shot him a speaking glance as she eased the big truck into the covered garage. She took a deep breath.

"Come on, your room is 301 a corner suite with pool access, weight room and sauna. Room service is twenty-four hours. Dial 9 for front desk, 7 for room service. Your bags will be brought to your room in five minutes." As she talked, she walked him to the elevator, handed him the two room keys. He noticed her mood shift from being teasing to all business. He bet she was hell in a boardroom.

Monday down bright and warm sun light streaming across Derek's face he smiled in his sleep reaching out for Ticara. Finding the bed empty he sat up abruptly looking around for her. He jumped from the bed and went to her bathroom to find a note on the mirror.

"Your first meeting is at ten o'clock this morning. Nykayla will be over to take you to town. I've gone to work and will see you at lunch. Love TiCara."

He smiled and went to get his clothes only to find she had already laid out his suit and shoes. All he had to do was shower, shave, and get ready. He laughed to himself, "yes I'm in love." The spray from the shower woke him up completely. The water felt like needles when it hit spots that TiCara had left with her little nails and her sucking lips. He smiled and enjoyed the sting of each little bit of water as he remembered how he got them.

By the time he was putting away his breakfast dishes Nykayla walked into the house with Teague following close on her heels. He greeted them both happily. Teague gave him a puzzled look as his eyes scanned the large living room and kitchen. As all three sat on the stools that surrounded the breakfast bar Nykayla briefed them on the people they would be meeting with. Their names, businesses, hobbies she gave them the full background even their families leaving out nothing.

Nykayla spoke as she stood there looking all business. He hair was a dark brown mass of curls pulled back from her face, except for a few escaping curls at her temples. He watched the well turned out attire, a knee length burnt orange skirt was topped by an autumn patterned top cinched around her waist by a dark brown belt that matched her Jimmi Choo pumps.

The person Teague met Sunday evening was gone and in her place was someone even more intriguing than the other. "Damn was he following in his little brother's footsteps or was it something in the air?" he thought to himself watching her hands move to make her point. He was so taken with watch her he didn't hear the last thing she said. Nykayla and Derek looked at each other with a shake of her head she walked up to him and clapped her hands in his face. He jumped back. He laughed at himself.

"Whoopee Damn, I was gone then Kayla. I'm sorry. My mind had wandered off. Must be something in the water, air, or something. Shit that never happened before." He wiped his hands down his face. Nykayla shook her head again after giving him a knowing smile.

"As I was saying before we zoned off. Bennett and Homel will be the two who will give you any problems. They will want to make a personal profit out of this and will bring up zoning and permit laws. That what you have me for. It won't take them long to look into your business ventures and try to squeeze you." Nykayla went on to the clue them in on Bennett's construction company and Homel's asphalt and paving business just to give them heads up on the two. She advised them to do their own research on the businesses and make their own decisions. After the meeting Kayla gave Teague the car keys.

"Here you go. The car is a hotel courtesy for all VIP guests." She smiled at him as she slid her laptop into her briefcase and closing it. "Alright gentlemen let's hit it!" She said grabbing a key off of the wall rack on her way out the back door. The brothers followed behind her. They waited until she had locked up. They went to the grey Lincoln LX parked in the drive. The garage doors opened slowly to reveal Kayla sitting up high in the driver's seat of a maroon Hummer.

"Damn!" Teague said as he eased the Lincoln out of the driveway to let her out. He fell in behind her as she hit the road. Derek smiled at his brother. "Keepers or throw them back?" he asked amused at Teague's expression.

"Keepers! These two are sho nuff keepers. Trophy catches. Man, two trophy catches." Teague laughed shaking his head in amazement. Derek laughed at Teague's excitement.

"I thought so. I thought so." He sat back in his seat to enjoy the ride. "First business then pleasures." He thought as he watched taillights of the Hummer. TiCara's soft giggles resounded in is mind. She was never far from his thoughts. "How could someone so small have so much power over him?" Another voice in his mind chimed in, "slow down bro, slow down. Don't know enough about her. You already in deep don't bury yourself dick first."

After leaving the Jolly Bro Giants Nykayla decided to do a lot more digging into their business practices and their personal lives. "Daddy you've always said if it looks too good it's hiding something. I'm gonna find out." She whispers to herself thinking it might be too late to save TiCara from heartache, but she be damned if she sat back and do nothing like she did the last time. No fucking way. Cara was family. Her responsibility since she was seven years old and that was the only time, she hadn't been there to protect her little friend. She blamed herself for all TiCara had went through. Never, never, never gain she had promised herself, her father, and most of all TiCara's unconscious body lying in the ICU.

After spending a couple of days in the two women's company Teague felt he had pretty much gotten an idea of their friendship. Nykayla was five years older than Ticara and she was the Truth, the big sister. The mastermind, the instigator, interrogator, protector, and provider. Mostly the bully and she didn't try to hide or justify her attitude. Ticara was genuine as she appeared. Mischievous and engaging, analytical, proper and demur. He shyness concealed a sharp mind and mean temper.

The two of them made an odd couple to say the least, but it fit. Nykayla was tall at least 5'10 well-toned body that she wasn't afraid to show off. She wore some outrageous hair styles and colors that let him know it was all weaves. He wondered what her real hair looked like. TiCara was very small framed about 5ft if she was an inch. Well-built easy on the eye. She wore a short pixie hair style that made him think of Tinker Bell. He liked the way she seemed to flutter around and the way his little brother hovered protectively around her.

He had witnessed enough that the report no longer mattered as much. He was convinced his brother had found a true diamond this time. Now if only he could take care of his itch for that long-legged powder keg that constantly teased and taunted his senses. Being left alone with her was not an option the temptation was too great. He tried his best not to be alone with her for more than a few minutes. She found that to be amusing.

The girl was deadly in the board room and the dance floor. She had taken them out to dinner then dancing at The Legends Lounge. Man, he had a good time. He had noticed that to his surprise his little brother could get down to some down-home blues. His little Tinkerbell Ticara didn't miss a beat either.

On the dance floor tell me that girl couldn't make a bulldog kiss a cat. The tempo of the music changed from a shake what your momma gave you to an old school bump and grind. This time he challenged her. She gave him a soft knowing smile and stepped into his arms.

Teague knew she was perfect, she fit. Her body her mind even that fit, the protective spirit that she had. Lost in the feel of her body moving against his, he knew she would be a perfect match for him in the bedroom also.

Nykayla's thoughts were the same as his, but she knew it was too soon for her to get attached. Fuck around with yeah. This brother had an overpowering chemistry that scared the shit out of her. She closed her eyes enjoying the feel of his big body moving slow and seductively against hers. She was getting wetter and wetter. Her nipples were hard as pebbles of granite. When he put his big hand behind her head in her hair long fingers massaged her neck and scalp, her body reacted instantly.

Nykayla swore she orgasmed right then and there on the dance floor. As she listened to his thudding heart race, he pulled her head back. She looked up into his eyes. The darkness seemed to boil. "Yes, kitten let go, I gottcha." He whispered to her. Nykayla's legs trembled. Her heart raced madly. Her only thought was to get away from this foot too damn good brother. She pushed against his chest trying to catch her breath, eyes cloudy with desire she cleared her throat." I've… I've got to go." Was all she could say before pulling away and rushing to the bathroom.

Ticara and Derek watched from their booth. She followed her and Derek followed Teague who had walked out of the door.

"Kay, you alright? Ticara asked as she sat beside Nykayla on the settee in the waiting room. Thank God the bathrooms were empty. Nykayla looked stunned and shaken. Seeing the concern on her little friends face she laughed.

"I thought you were in trouble, man! That brotha is dangerous. Lil bro ain't got nothing. I mean nothing on Big Bro." She said nervously her hands trembling as she took a deep breath. TiCara laughed and continued listening.

"I mean the dude made me bust a nut just dancing. What the fuck? I've never felt like that, on fire and freezing. What? I wanted to run away and stick closer all at the same time. Damn!" Nykayla exclaimed frustrated getting more so at the sound of TiCara's giggles.

"Well," said TiCara, "an ole lady once told me to take a chance. Get your fuck on and see where it leads." She gave Nykayla's advice back to her. "It can't be that bad."

Nykayla looked at her as if she had been slapped. "Bad! Bad! If that is his foreplay shit, I'll be dead before he gets to his business." She corrected shaking her head to try and chase the chills away. TiCara sat beside her and gave her a tight hug.

"Let's go." She said getting up pulling Kayla with her.

"Where?" Asked Kayla standing up as commanded.

"To ride the wave." TiCara responded.

To Ride the Wave, was the name of their joint business in Biloxi and Mobile that catered to the rich and famous. Nykayla knew TiCara wasn't talking about business. She rolled her neck cracking it like a boxer loosening up.

"Alright, bring it on big boy. Mama coming to see bout ya." She joked. TiCara laughed as they walked out of the waiting room back into the club.

Derek found Teague leaning against the side of the building. He watched him for a few minutes before approaching. He knew his brother knew he was there before he could say anything. Teague turned on him.

"Alright she's gotten to me. I don't know how, but she had.' He confided rubbing his hand down his face. "Man, I just wanted to wrap her in my arms and fuck her brains out, and then I feel this need to protect her. There is something about her that has me tied in fucking knots. Damn this is off, ya know. I don't know if I should run or stay." He was confused about these mixed emotions. It was more than just sex even though he knew it would be explosive.

Derek wanted to laugh, but he didn't.

"Well Big T all I can tell you is just let it happen and be ready to admit it is what it is." He advised him never having seen his brother bothered by nothing. He always seemed unfadeable until now. These dirty south females were hell on a brother's confidence. They could lift him up so high he could touch the moon. His grandfather used to say, "the harder the nut the sweeter the meat inside."

"Nut cracking time." He told his brother with a chuckle. Teague had to laugh at his little brother using their grandfather's fight phrase. Hell, he could handle Nykayla. He'd met way more woman who were beautiful and sexy as hell. He didn't have a problem with them. He'd just treated her like one of them. He'd be alright.

They got back to the booth before the ladies and ordered fresh drinks. The remainder of the evening Teague and Nykayla played cat and mice. Derek and Ticara watched with interest the bold advances and strategic retreats. Ticara leaned into Derek's chest and whispered, "I'm really horny Big Daddy take me home." Her sweet breath made his dick jump. Her soft words made him hard.

"What took you so long?" He whispered back. She nodded her head toward Teague and Nykayla and raised her eyebrows. He smiled. "They're older than we are. They can handle themselves." He answered her unspoken question holding her hand he stood up.

"See you all in the morning for church." He told them taking their leave and the two of them left the other two at the table. Nykayla laughed looking a little more in control Teague holding her hand in both of his.

"What happens now?" He asked her. Nykayla leaned closer to him. The seriousness in his voice touched something inside of Nykayla causing that I'm in control part of her take over. She stood up looking down at him.

"I guess we're gonna have to ride the wave and find out." She said seductively. Teague stood also after leaving a ten-dollar tip on the table.

"I don't get it." He replied hoping his thoughts were right. Going outside he opened the door of the Lincoln for her then got in himself.

"I don't want to assume anything Nykayla I want to hear it out of your mouth. Okay, I know what I want, but I need to know if you want the same thing." He told her needing to hear her say she wanted him. He knew he could easily persuade her and arouse her to the point where he could have her, but he wanted her to want him freely.

"Teague, I know I want you and any fool with eyes can see you want me. We are two grown people. I want to make love to you, or we can just sit around frustrating the hell out of each other. Which one do you prefer?" She asked running her well-manicured hand up and down his thick thigh inching closer and closer towards his crotch. Teague licked his lips and exhaled heavily.

"You gonna let me have you, no regrets?" He asked looking into her green eyes.

"No never have me only borrow." She leaned over he closed the space between them, meeting her lips hungrily.

Lord she'd been wanting to taste his lips since the first met at the airport. It was worth the wait. She sighed heavily pulling away she sat back in her seat quickly.

"Let's go." She ordered tensely he laughed at her expression. She looked how he felt tied in knots.

At the room Teague didn't hesitate to draw her into his arms he devoured her mouth. He wanted to build her up and ease her down. He did repeatedly, kissing and caressing. Kayla didn't know when or how but all their clothes were off. Teague laid her on the large bed. On his knees he kissed her pussy lips causing darts of excitement to rush her nerves. He loved her so intensely Kayla didn't realize she was screaming his name.

Teague kissed his way up her body admiring the beautiful skin that felt like silk to touch. He was determined to touch every part of her tonight. His hands roamed over his head and shoulders as he moved up to look in her face. He just looked trying to store away memories for later. She looked up at him and a smile touched her lips with a sudden push she had him on his back and was intent on having her way with him. She shimmed down his long hard body nibble here nibble there causing him to grunt or groan as if he was in pain.

Kayla smiled and said, "you ain't felt noting yet." She thought to herself as she reached her target. Feeling the enormous dick, she was in shock. Taking in a started gulp of air as she looked at it. It was a good ten inches and so damned thick. Nykayla pulled back instinctively looking up to see him watching her closely.

"I know it's big, but it won't bite unless you want it to." He whispered to her. It was now or never. Nykayla looked at him unsure of how to proceed.

"I… um… I know I have a big mouth, but this." She said waving the head at him, "is a hell of a big bite." She looked back at the enormous head that seemed to taunt and dare her. Teague remained silent letting her make up her mind. When he felt the first attentive touch of her lips touch his base right above his balls, he didn't realize he was holding his breath until it swished out loudly.

Nykayla giggled as she nibbled her way up the thick main vein. She flicked her tongue around the crease of the head making his big body jerk. Once she made it to the head, she played with his balls caressing pulling and squeezing them gently. Her tongue was busy playing with the opening dipping in to feel and taste the baby soft skin. Opening her mouth wide she took him in little by little she sucked as much as she thought she could take. When his large hands grabbed the back of her head and started pumping into her mouth. Nykayla fought the urge to throw up as his dick pumped passed the back of her throat.

She pushed against his thick thighs struggling to get up, her frantic movement snapped him back. He pulled her up against his chest holding her close, he rained kisses on her face and neck. "I'm sorry... so sorry." He repeated over and over so he kissed her throat he aroused her until she couldn't think straight. Rolling her over he spread her legs bending her knees on each side of his wide frame. He settled in the cradle of her bent knees.

"Kayla, kitten I need to know now, Can I, have you? Last chance to back out." He whispered praying she would go for it. Nykayla looked into his cool black eyes the heat that radiated from them was scorching.

"For now, let's ride the tide." She whispered reaching between them she placed his dick head in the opening of her pussy slowly moving her hips adjusting to his thickness. Eyes locked he began to inch his way into her tightness pumping slowly and deep. The pain was blinding. She shut her eyes tight biting her lips so hard she could taste blood.

"Loosen up kitten, ya killing me." He whispered going deep grunting. Lord he was big breathing deeply Nykayla forced her body to relax releasing the tension in her muscles.

"Ahh... yes kitten let me in." He encouraged as he sunk deeper. The feel of her muscles massaging squeezing him was testing his will power.

"Move... I... Move..." She urged him not waiting she began to move against him wrapping her legs around his waist. She pulled him deeper with each move. Teague held his weight off of her. He didn't dare move to engulfed in watching her as she pumped and grind against him.

He waited tensely until he could feel her climax getting close. He moved. Encircling her with his arms he let the sensation take over. He plowed into her hard and fast. He couldn't stop now if he had to. He pumped into her hot pussy so hard and fast. The headboard banged against the wall. Nykayla could only hold on and beg for more.

"Harder Tee harder." She cheered him on as he pounds into her so hard, he was lifting her off of the bed. She clung to him giving as much as she got.

Teague put her legs on his shoulder leaned over her gripped the headboard. He felt like his heart was going to burst as he pounded harder trying to get closer to her. The pressure was building and building. Nykayla couldn't stand anymore. Throwing her head back the climax took her breath. Teague knowing, he was about to explode released her legs and held on to her as he frantically pumped into her. He buried his face in her shoulder as they cried out in ecstasy. They both were flying and tumbling through the sky.

"Hold me kitten. Just hold me." He whispered against her neck. Nykayla still clung to him she was too afraid to let go even as Teague rolled over off of her. Sleep claimed them as their hearts slowed to its normal rhythm and their breathing slowly eased up. Nykayla mumbled in her sleep Teague curved his big body around her as sleep claimed him.

Nykayla woke up around four thirty in the morning stretching and arching her back in a feline manner. The tingle in her pussy made her smile. Rolling on her side she inspected the supersized brotha beside her. Even in his sleep he commanded attention. Nykayla let her eyes travel over his face. His brother, Derek, was male-model handsome. The face she was examining was anything but. His was a strong face that spoke of solidness, maturity and protection a lot of the things she had needed but never found in one man. The fact that he could fuck a sista's brains out was a big plus.

As if his body was responding to her thoughts his dick started to harden. Nykayla watched as it hardened at the base that was nestled in curly black hairs to half mass. She couldn't resist reaching out to touch it. Cool long fingers wrapped around him. Tague grunted in his sleep. Nykayla eased down in the bed peeking through his hair to see if he was awake. She sucked the harmless looking head into her mouth. The more she tasted the more she wanted. His big body responded to her instinctively pumping in and out. Taking a deep breath through her nose she was determined to swallow this beast. The head pushed pass her gag reflex and she sucked harder as he pumped into her making smacking slurping sounds. She could feel him getting ready to unload reaching under her chin she grabbed his balls squeezing them until he shouted.

"Kitten please... I'm cumming... Kitten!" He shouted her name grabbing her head he humped frantically banging her face against his pelvic. Nykayla's sharp nails it into his thick thighs as his dick showered his throat.

"Good, God, Kitten. Jesus Christ you trying to kill me." He said pulling his dick out of her mouth. He lifter her up to face him. He looked at her shaking his head from side to side in wonder. She had just done something no woman had ever done to him. He pulled her close kissing her Kayla was so turned on. She would have tried to take him in the ass, but she knew somethings had to take time.

His large fingers fucked her wet pussy until she was cumming back-to-back. Teague laid her on her stomach on a pillow lifting that fine ass in the air. The round cheeks looked too damned good. He kissed and bit them making her cry out. Sitting on his knees he rubbed his thick dick head at her pink pussy opening thinking how good it felt inside. Then his thoughts turned to how the hell a hole that small can open up for a dick as big as his. This wasn't a dream it was too real. He was going to enjoy it while it lasted. Pushing the head in slowly. He watched pumping slowly as inch by inch he disappeared grabbing her ass cheeks he spread them wide.

Her tight ass hole peeked at him licking his fingers he leaned into her and whispered, "Are you ready for a little extra? I've got something for you." Slipping his finger up her ass. Nykayla screamed as she nutted, burying her face in the pillow. Her ass bucking against him. Loosing herself in the wave, she screamed, "Harder Tee harder. Ride it. Oh God I'm cumming. Tee." She cried trying to get away from the intense heat.

He grabbed her waist and pumped and grounded into her until his nuts were slapping against her pussy. Their harsh tortured breathing climax to roars and squelches as each of them erupted in a shattering orgasm. They collapsed on the bed each soaking wet, breathing hard, neither able to speak only look at each other in awe.

Back to Business

Personally, things were going well on the business side. Proof of land ownership came up challenging Nykayla's thirty acers. It didn't take long for her to show proof of ownership, grievance about the sale of the land citing it to be Heir Property. Every challenge Nykayla met and defeated. Some were dealt with through her lawyer some through fiery confrontation. She would not be hindered.

Teague attended ever meeting and was suitably impressed with her there was no question about it the girl was bad. She could be gently reassuring to downright cutthroat. As he found out in her last confrontation. Teague had tagged a car following them for two days in a row. Nykayla asked him to pull into a service station which he did sure enough. The small pickup pulled in behind them. Teague intended to find out who, what, and why were they following them. Before he could say anything Nykayla got out of the car stormed over to the truck snatching the driver's door open.

"What the hell is this about Nevells?" She yelled angrily as the man seemed to unfold himself out of the truck. A tall pasty dark skinned and crack-head thin man straightens his shoulders.

"You know that's our family's land. You got no right to sell it without all of our say so." He yelled back pointing his finger in her face. Nykayla slapped his hand away not backing down.

"No, it's mine, my father bought it for my sixteenth birthday. I got the papers to prove it. Ya'll aint never had nothing but that little nasty juke joint. If you keep fucking with me, you won't have that." She shouted back stepping to him. She was aware of his tendency to slap a woman around. She silently wished he would try her. She hated all of those people. The Outlaws and Brackton's, they were nothing but trouble.

His body tensed in a threatening manner. Nykayla tensed, Teague watched leaning against the Lincoln with his arms folded across his massive chest.

"You ain't nothing but a bastard. Chile, you Daddy made my aunt into a hoe and never gave her a dime just so you could steal our land. If'n it wuz'n fo that bitch he wuz married to we'd have all of it. Ya'll killed Eddie ta keep it, but he'd gave it back fo ya killed im." Nevell's spat at her angrily.

Nykayla had had enough. She hit the guy in the

face so hard blood spurted down his shirt. Grabbing his face, he looked at her menacing. Upon seeing his blood, he seemed to lose it. Roaring he charged Nykayla who held her ground. Teague start to intervene just as Nykayla punched him. He had heard enough. Before he got to them the man roared and charged.

Nykayla grabbed his outstretched arm and sent him flying over her head onto the gravel parking lot. Teague froze as she kicked off her heel and bounced around rolling her head from side to side popping her neck. Teague grinned at the sight she made standing like a boxer wearing a twelve-hundred-dollar Vera Wang suit. Not a hair out of place, her makeup was flawless as she danced around in stockinged feet.

Come on Cracker Jack that's all you are. A poor excuse for a man to beat up on a woman. All ya'll sorry assed Low lives are alike. You, your brothers, you sorry as pappy and your tired ass cousins. Beat up on me, Trick. I got something for yo ass." She taunted him.

Nevells got up off the ground and charged her again. Teague watched Nykayla jump in the air turn sideways and kick the brotha in the face sending him crashing to the ground with a thud.

Time to stop this Teague told himself. Walking up to her, he put his arm around her shoulders. "That's enough Kitten calm down." He whispered to her. The only time he called her that was in bed, yet it rolled off of his tongue so easily now. She must have realized it too, because the tension was released from her immediately as she leaned into him. His solidness was her comfort.

Teague eyed the man as he struggled to his feet. "You should be smart to stop making trouble or the next time you might have to tangle with me." He threw the guy a couple of tens and walked Nykayla into the service station. The two young women that worked there gave her a high five on the way to the bathroom.

Teague asked had the incident been recorded. They nodded, and he offered to pay for the tape. After securing the tape he chatted with them finding out more about the man Nykayla just beat down. They offered him an earful and none of it good. When asked about the Eddie person they didn't know much about him jus that he died in a really bad car wreck some years ago. It all gave him something to think about and look into.

Nykayla had a bad feeling about this altercation. She knew Teague would have a lot of questions about what he'd heard. Surprisingly, he didn't mention it and that made her worry even more. Teague took his suspicions and his dossier to Derek two days later as they sat in the boardroom for their final meeting.

Derek sat at the end of a long oak table reading over some pricing specs. Nodding to himself in satisfaction he sat back in the chair with a little smile. After this final closing meeting he had planned to take a week off to celebrate. Ticara had promised to come home with him to meet his family. To him it was a win-win all sales would be final and filed.

He got the property he wanted and most of all the woman he needed to make his life complete. Wo could ask for more. He smiled to himself. He tapped his feet impatiently wanting to be TiCara , just the thought of her slow sneaky smile made his heart jerk in his chest. He couldn't wait to take her home to show her his favorite places, his friends, and his lake house. She would be his for a whole week. No business, no Teague or Nykayla must the two of them.

Teague interrupted his wandering thoughts with a loud ahh huh! Looking up at him, Derek shook his hand and laughed.

"Man, I'll be glad when this is over. McIntyre's here". He asked about their lawyer.

"Yeah, he's here. He got in last night. Look man we need to talk before everyone gets here. I should have said something days ago, but I had to look into a few things first." Teague said messaging the back of his neck to try to ease the tension that had built over the last couple of days. He dropped a manilla envelope in front of Derek who looked from the envelope to his brother. A feeling of dread crawled down his spine pushing the envelope away from him, he stood up looking at Teague questioning.

"What the hell is this? Man, I don't want to know what's in there do I?" He was looking at the envelope with TiCara's name and the name of one of their Private Investigator's logo on it.

"You just can't let me be happy, can you? You got to find something to bitch about, don't you?" Derek turned his chair over, slamming it to the floor staring at Teague in disbelief and hurt and fury. Teague opened the envelope pulled out a copy of Eddie Brackton's accident report and death certificate. The accident report held a lot of question marks. The death certificate stated undetermined due to the conditions of the remains.

A copy of TiCara's grandparent last Will and Testament, her only surviving relative was Ny'kayla Carmel Brackton Westbrook. The two women named were mentioned together with property estate and a few questionable transactions. The girl didn't look as clean as they appeared.

Derek didn't hear anything pass undetermined. He already knew the story. The fact that the bastard's family was crying foul play made his blood boil. Closing his eyes in blinding anger he yelled,"

"Enough! I don't care. That bastard deserved more than he got. So, don't come telling me what those wanna be Ballers got to say. You hear me? Shut the fuck up." He stood face to face with Teague fire blazing out of his eyes. Teague fired blazing out of his eyes. Teague not backing down yelled back.

"Damn it man! Are you that damned whipped that you can't see what's in front of you? They are trying to set us up just like they did to that poor Eddie fellow." As the brother's argued they didn't notice Ticara and Nykayla had walked into the room until Teague spoke Eddie's name. A sharp sound of wounded pain escaped Ticara's mouth. Nykayla hugged her close. She struggled to get free like a trapped animal.

"Cara, wait." Derek shouted trying to get to her. She bolted the door. Kayla blocked him from following. Now the side of Nykayla's personality surfaced that she was always struggling to control. With a dark deadly command, she ordered them to shut up and sit. Derek looking around frantically said, "What have you done man? What have you done?

"You've killed me. Man, you've killed me." He sat mumbling to himself tears ran down his face. Teague stood looking everywhere but at Kayla, who took over.

"What happened to her husband? Why does it say undetermined? Shit she didn't even go to the poor bastard's funeral." He asked pointing to the papers on the table. Knowing with a sinking heart he had messed up.

"He killed his own dammed self. Alcohol, too

many Viagra's and just being fucking evil. If I knew half of what he had been doing to my baby, he would have been dead a long fucking time before that. You want to know why she didn't go to the funeral? Fine, I'll show you. Don't move stay right there." She ordered leaving out of the room only to return in less than five minutes.

In her hand she held a thick folder. Opening the folder, she began to throw pictures on the table. Pictures she refused to look at. "This is why she didn't show her last respects to the sorry waste of God's good air. Look at them damn it!" She almost screamed grabbing a picture off the table that showed TiCara's mangled body laying tossed like a rag doll at the foot of their stairs. No clothing, covered only in bruises, gashes, bite marks and blood. She shoved it in Teague's face. Grabbing the doctor's report, she shoved it at him also. Teague grabbed the picture and the report.

"Read and look until your heart is content. Another thing we don't need to set you up. For what? We have our own. My father took care of that. You and your brother are only worth a couple hundred million. Well Hello Bitch! My niece and I together are billionaires many times over. We don't need you or your change. All negotiations are off from this point forward. All your change will be returned even for your stay here will be refunded. Take all of your shit and get out of my hotel in two hours or you will be escorted out. That concludes our business Sir's."

With that she turned and walked out of the room. Leaving the two brothers alone Derek could only moan and sob. The pictures of TiCara's broken mangled body tore his heart out. The attending doctor wrote the here injuries were consistent with being attacked by a pack of wild dogs. Chances of recovery slim, not conceivable.

Derek threw up on the floor. Teague was silenced by shame looking at his baby brother suffering bowels rise in his throat.

"How could a man do this to a beautiful… Lord. She doesn't even look human." He was so stunned. Anger began to rise up in him. He listened to those lying bastards down in the bottoms well if he had to lose all he had then they would lose something too.

"Derek man, I'm sorry. I'll make this right I promise; on all I love… I'll make it right. I'll find TiC…" Teague was slammed against the wall. Derek pinned him there looking up in his eyes with deadly intent.

"Don't you go near her. Do... don't even say her name. Understand? You've done more than enough." Derek released him and ran out the room. Teague gathered all the photos and reports calming himself as he kept his hands busy. Putting everything in a neat pile he put them in a folder Ny'Kayla had brought in.

"Well Mr.Brackton, I told you if you lied you would pay and it's time to pay up." He said to the empty room carrying the folder with him. He pulled out his cell phone called his lawyer to warm him later that evening to bond him out of jail.

The Aftermath

Derek found TiCara a few minutes after Nykayla did. In his heart he knew where she would go a tender soul as she was. He pulled up to the gates of the huge cemetery that laid on the back of the southside of town. Slowly he made his way to the four large headstones that made up TiCara's family. Hearing their soft-spoken words, he stopped. It reminded him of their first physical meeting by the pool. He only prayed this meeting would turn out like a fraction of that one.

He stepped around her grandfather's huge headstone, the two women looked up at him. No shock or surprise on their faces. Anger and disgust written on Nykayla's face. Ticara was as blank and closed off as the graves she sat on. Nykayla stood up and stepped in front of her.

"What do you want now?" she demanded. Her eyes cutting into him. Holding up his hands he took a deep breath.

"I want TiCara. I want her now and forever. Teague didn't believe all that shit; he was doing what you are doing Kayla. What you've been doing all your life, protecting her. He was protecting me. He's my big brother it's his job just like your niece was yours." He told her as simply as he could. TiCara had come to her feet.

"You hurt my baby. I won't tolerate it, do you hear me? She's all that I have, and I'll die before I see her torn up again get it!" I let her down. I let that animal almost kill her. I won't let it happen again." Speaking slowly, tears running down her face. She felt TiCara's small arms wrap around her giving her a squeeze.

"It's okay Tee Tee. I'm a big girl now. I knew one day he would hear all those lies. I just hoped he would love me enough not to listen. You didn't let me down you forced me to confront my fears and live my dream." She laughed softly. "It was awesome, and I thank you, Pawpaw would be proud of you." Ticara smiled sadly exhaled loudly turned to face Derek her eyes just as bright as ever.

"I don't know what to say to you. I know you didn't dig up that mess about me, and I want to believe you didn't believe any of it. And no, I will not defend myself against any of it. I have no reason to. A lie can't stand on its own. It has to have others to hold it up.'

"Derek regardless of what Teague's PI's may have told him none of it is based on facts except

Nykayla being my aunt. Which isn't a secret. She is my Pawpaw's daughter and mama loved her as if she was hers. I love her because she is mine just like I love you. It won't cost you nothing. The devil has put me through hell, but God's love only made me stronger. I forgave Eddie. It still hurts but I had to forgive him. If I hadn't God never would have sent you to me. I thank Him every day and tell Teague I forgive him also. I understand why he did what he did. Where is he anyway?" She asked concerned.

Over the last six weeks she had some to see him as her big silent friend. 'she had hoped he would like to be her uncle. "Oh well, can't change the world in a day." She thought to herself shrugging her shoulders as if to say to hell with it.

Nykayla was so proud of her niece. She handled this with so much grace and class. Now she knew she had to let her go. She had grown up on her and she hadn't even noticed it. Too busy being a bully and overprotective aunt. Well look how good she turned out. I didn't do too bad," she thought to herself with satisfaction. She looked around and saw TiCara in Derek's arms. She smiled. "Good job Kay, Good job Daddy is proud of you girlie." She heard her father's voice say to her.

Derek was holding TiCara so close his tears rain down over her head. His heart was so full and grateful. He didn't know what he had did to deserve her. He wasn't going to let her go. He felt a sharp slap on his arm lifting his head his eyes met Nykayla's with a smile of forgiveness on her face.

"Come on Crybaby we've got to go get your brother. He's down in the bottoms tearing down folks' shit." Nykayla laughed hurrying to her car. TiCara climbed up into her Hummer shaking her head. Derek ran to the Lincoln falling in line behind the girls. Damn they drove like bats out of hell.

Derek thought to himself as he floored the Lincoln giving chase through the back streets of the friendly city. Teague's path of destruction in the bottoms was easy to follow. Police cars, fire trucks, and ambulances blocked the street on each corner. Nykayla got there first making a beeline for Lieutenant Jones.

"Lieutenant what's happened?" Please tell me he hasn't killed anybody yet?" She gripped his chubby forearm he laughed and patted her hand.

"Well seems like them Brackton's and Outlaw's has put their stuff on the wrong fella this time. He was looking for the one named Nevell. When no one would tell him where he was, he tore down every shack on the row. Then he went over to the lil' Juke Joint and tossed everyone out. Nevell was hiding in the attic and wouldn't come out so this Big Ass Umbrae wrapped a chain around the support beams, hooked to the back of that big rig.

"He's going to pull... Ahhh... shit... there it goes." Lieutenant Jones yelled excitedly. The noise was tremendous. Screaming, siren and crumbling buildings. Ny'kayla and Derek rushed to the truck pushing past policemen and spectators. Teague waved at them from the cab with a big grin on his face. He climbed down out of the truck. Nykayla ran into his arms. The city and county police force were out in full force. Guns down looking confused in the mix of the chaos.

Teague walked to the street with his hands in the air getting on his knees he clamped his hands behind his back assuming the position of surrender.

In the News

Breaking news at six. Florida Millionaire Developer goes berserk. "Teague Cumpton, a Florida Developer demolished a small community called the Bottoms area this afternoon. No reason had been given for the rampage. Suspect have himself up. City and County police were on the scene. Six injuries reported to be non-life threatening. Only one person was taken to the hospital, and has since been released with a broken arm, leg, and jaw. Nevell Brackton, shown here refused to speak to Reporters or Officers in charge of the incident, all he would say was quote. "That damned Haitian is crazy." More as news becomes available.

Sitting on the loveseat in TiCara's large den, Teague watched himself wave at Nykayla and Derek, as they ran toward the large truck. He laughed at how silly he looked. All his life he had been conscious of public appearances. All that flew out of the window when intentional lies had hurt his brother and two of the most genuine females he had ever met.

Released on a two hundred-thousand-dollar bond Nykayla had brought him to TiCara's house. Derek and their lawyers had handled all the legal work. None of the residents wanted to press charges. The property owner refused to press so the city sited him for felonious mischief, endangering the life of Civilians, and Officers. Teague didn't really care because he had made sure no one was in the building. He ran through. He had only wanted Nevells. Once they realized he meant to run through every structure in the Bottoms until he found him, they gave him up. Hiding in a little ragged club house called BeeBee's Beehive with his family and flunkies guarding him.

Teague had made short work of them all. Nevelle's had hid in the attic since he wouldn't come down and Teague was too big to fit in the crawl space. He decided to being the whole place down and he did. "What on earth made you destroy all those houses?" Asked Kayla already knowing the answer.

"That day you whipped him up, you said something about their juke joint. I decided to make your threat into a promise. I looked into his business and found out he owned those little trap houses. I don't know, I felt like his lies had caused me to lose all I loved. He loved money so I made sue he lost just as much. "He laughed at himself.

His cellphone ranged again. He glanced at it. His mother was calling again for the eighth time he let it ring. Nykayla and TiCara looked at him in amusement.

TiCara's phone ranged she stepped out of the room to answer it. She giggled as she hung up and walked back into the room. "Come on big boy. Time to face the music." She patted his shoulder headed for the front door just as the doorbell ranged out. She opened the door. Teague and Nykayla walked up behind her. Standing at the door was his mother and father and Derek McIntyre.

"Hello mother, father," Teague greeted them shamefully. The small-framed woman with a silvery gray hair rushed in hugging this man who seemed twice her size. She went from a concerned mother hen to an angry demon in a blink of an eye. She started smacking him on the arm and shoulders.

"Why did you do this? You scared us to death Just like your father, hot headed." She spoke with a soft island accent. The large man came to his rescue, lifting the lady off of him.

"Son, I tried to tell her you were alright, she

wouldn't hear it. She had to get here and see for herself." The large man said the sound seemed to come from his bell and roll its way out of his mouth. Cordial Cumpton was even taller than his sons and almost as wide, while their mother fell in between Nykayla's 5'10 and TiCara's 5", slim but beautifully build, olive skin, stately green eyes that for a moment looked like a storm.

Tricia Cumpton was a force to be reckoned with and it looked like her men knew it. Teague looked to Nykayla for help. She laughed and took charge of the situation. After introduction, she had seated and served everyone. They laughed and talked for hours. Everyone got comfortable and friendly. Tricia started advising the girls on how to keep her boys in line and make them behave. Cordial toured the house with Derek and Teague.

The evening ended peacefully with Tricia hugging both girls giving them a sly wink. Cordial hugged the girls thanked them for looking after his boys. On there way to the hotel Tricia stated,

"Is this gonna be a double wedding or separate?" speaking to Teague, who only groaned out loud and looking at his hands. Derek had stayed behind with TiCara, so he barely escaped.

Nykayla laughed and the girls talked in the back seat started back up with squeals and giggles.

Cordial patted his son on the thigh in sympathy.

THE END

Doris Jones